Joan Draper
267 Victoria St.
Niagara-on-the-
Lake, Ont
LOS1J0
1- ~~416~~ · 468·7885
    905·

My Commonplace Book.

1993

Y0-BPW-055

"I HAVE SOMETIMES DREAMT
THAT WHEN THE DAY OF
JUDGMENT DAWNS—
THE ALMIGHTY WILL TURN
TO ST. PETER AND WILL
SAY, WHEN HE SEES US
COMING WITH OUR BOOKS
UNDER OUR ARMS,

"LOOK THESE NEED NO
REWARD. WE HAVE NOTHING
TO GIVE THEM HERE. THEY
HAVE LOVED READING."

VIRGINIA WOOLF

He First Deceased,
She For A Little Tried
To Live Without Him,
Liked It Not,
And Died.

Upon the death of Sir Albert.
Morton's Wife - by Sir Henry
Wotton. 1627

Final Entry in D.C. Partridge
Her Book.

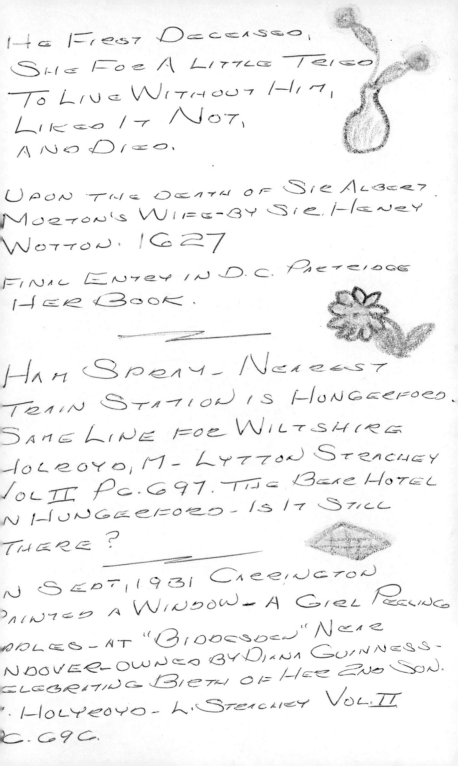

Ham Spray - Nearest
Train Station is Hungerford.
Same Line For Wiltshire
Holroyd, M - Lytton Strachey
Vol II Pg. 697. The Bear Hotel
N Hungerford - Is It Still
There?

N Sept, 1931 Carrington
Painted a Window - A Girl Peeling
Apples - at "Biddesden" Near
Ndover - Owned by Diana Guinness-
Celebrating Birth of Her 2nd Son.
'. Holyeoyo - L. Strachey Vol. II
C. 696.

Strachey, Lytton, Bronze
Plaque in Strachey Chapel,
Church St. Andrews,
Chew Magna, Somerset.

TLS July 24, 1992
Pg. 15. NB - Archive
Recordings of Virginia's
Cook, Lottie Hope
Reminiscing about Virginia
Radio 4's Art Magazine
Kaleidoscope

~

Edith Sitwell said "The Bloomsbury Group consists of
couples in Triangular arrangements
in Squares"
(living)

/

Vanity Fair by Thackeray
is indicative of Bloomsbury
in the 1850's.

Suggested Reading for
Bloomsbury in early 1800's
Henry Esmond - Thackeray
Little Dorrit - Dickens

Great literature makes one
detached and therefore braver,
less purely egocentric -
it helps us to abstain
from fear, from hatred,
from tribal religion.

Bio. of E. M. Forster by
Nicola Beaumann pg. 296.

Thanks to books, the dead appear
to me as though they still lived....
Everything decays and falls into dust
by force of time: Saturn is never
weary of devouring his children,
and the glory of the world would
be buried in oblivion, had not God
as a remedy conferred on mortal
man the benefit of books...
Books are the masters that
instruct us without rods or
ferules, without reprimand or
anger, without the solemnity of
the gown or the expense of lessons
go to them, you will not find them
asleep: if you err, no scoldings
on their part: if you are ignorant,
no mocking laughter.

Richard de Bury 1281-1345

Philobiblon, London 1888

See next page
re R. De Bury →

de Bury, Richard (1281-1345)

Named from his birthplace, Bury St. Edmonds. Was tutor to Edward III when Prince of Wales, became Bishop of Durham and is celebrated as a patron of learning. He was an ardent collector of books, employing for this purpose members of the Mendicant orders. He founded a library in Durham College, Oxford, and was author of "Philobiblon," the autobiographical sketch in Latin of a lover of letters, first printed in 1473. An English translation was published in 1832.

—————————⟶—————————

From Virginia Woolf's Diary:

"The truth is that writing is the profound pleasure and being read the superficial."

Quoted in Candia McWilliam's review of James King's Bio of Virginia Woolf
Sunday Independent Magazine
Aug. 28/94

VOL. II OF MICHAEL HOLROYD'S BIO
OF AUGUSTUS JOHN, PAGE 132 -
HENRY LAMB, IN 1918, LIVED AT
#10 HILL ST. IN POOLE. HE MOVED
THERE TO BE NEAR DORELIA JOHN.

WOOLF, VIRGINIA, BORN
JAN. 25, 1882 - DIED MAR. 28, 1941

LYTTON STRACHEY DIED
JAN. 21, 1932.

CARRINGTON DIED MAR. 11, 1932

HENRY LAMB LIVED AT #10
HILL ST, POOLE

AUGUSTUS JOHN'S HOME IN
PARKSTONE. ALDERNEY NOW A
METHODIST CHAPEL (1975)
JOHN DIED IN 1961. HIS WORK
FROM 1936-'61 IS NOT CONSIDERED
HIS BEST

"ON OR ABOUT 1910, HUMAN CHARACTER CHANGED".
VIRGINIA WOOLF WROTE AFTER SEEING FIRST POST IMPRESSIONIST EXHIBITION IN LONDON.

———

VIRGINIA WROTE TO CLIVE BELL IN 1927 AFTER HE WROTE HER AND PRAISED "TO THE LIGHTHOUSE".

"I MEANT NOTHING BY "TO THE LIGHTHOUSE"... I CAN'T MANAGE SYMBOLISM EXCEPT IN THIS VAGUE GENERALISED WAY. WHETHER IT'S RIGHT OR WRONG I DON'T KNOW; BUT DIRECTLY I'M TOLD WHAT A THING MEANS, IT BECOMES HATEFUL TO ME."

JOAN SAYS "HURRAH FOR VIRGINIA. MY FEELINGS EXACTLY."

QUENTIN BELL, IN HIS
BIOGRAPHY OF VIRGINIA
WOOLF (VOL. 2 PAGE 119)
REFERING TO VIRGINIA'S
RELATIONSHIP WITH VITA:

" SHE COULD NOT REALLY
LOVE WITHOUT FEELING
THAT SHE WAS IN THE
PRESENCE OF A SUPERIOR
INTELLECT ":